EASY PIANO

THE GREATEST
VIDEO GAME
MUSIC

ISBN 978-1-4950-8231-3

HAL•LEONARD®

For all works contained herein:
Unauthorized copying, arranging, adapting, recording, Internet posting, public performance,
or other distribution of the music in this publication is an infringement of copyright.
Infringers are liable under the law.

Visit Hal Leonard Online at
www.halleonard.com

Contact us:
Hal Leonard
7777 West Bluemound Road
Milwaukee, WI 53213
Email: info@halleonard.com

In Europe, contact:
Hal Leonard Europe Limited
42 Wigmore Street
Marylebone, London, W1U 2RN
Email: info@halleonardeurope.com

In Australia, contact:
Hal Leonard Australia Pty. Ltd.
4 Lentara Court
Cheltenham, Victoria, 3192 Australia
Email: info@halleonard.com.au

ANGRY BIRDS THEME

By ARI PULKKINEN

Moderately

Copyright © 2009 Rovio Entertainment Limited
All Rights Administered Worldwide by Kobalt Songs Music Publishing
All Rights Reserved   Used by Permission

5

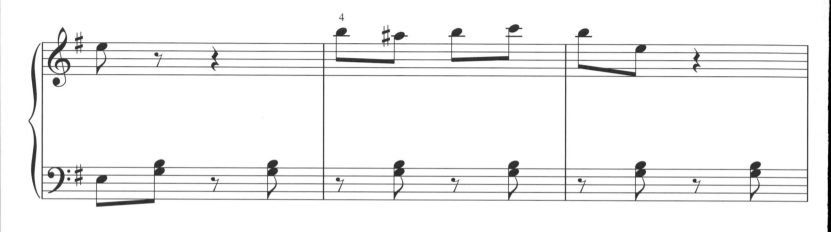

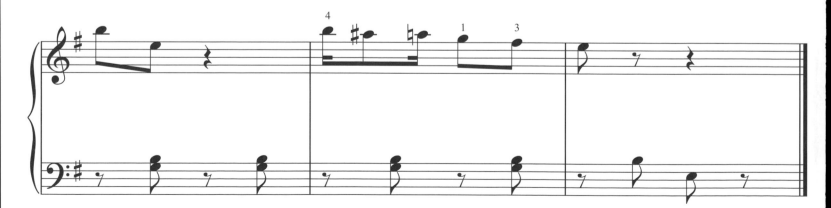

ASSASSIN'S CREED III MAIN TITLE

By LORNE BALFE

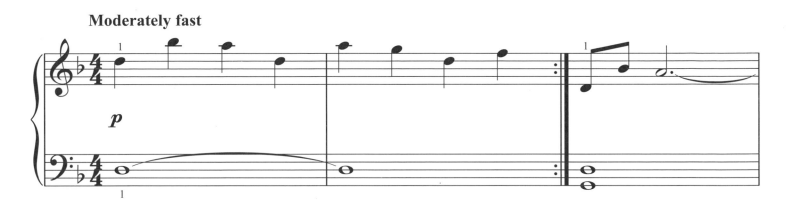

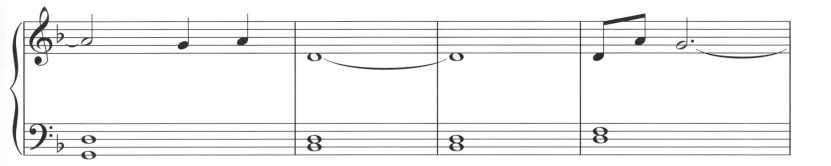

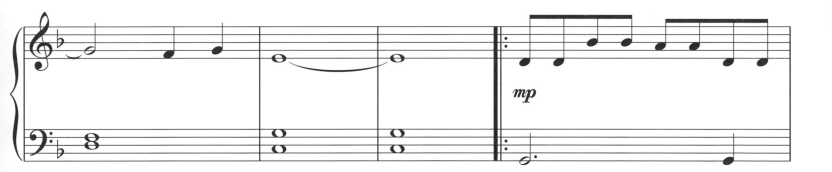

Copyright © 2013 by Ubisoft Editions Musique Inc.
All Rights in the United States Administered by Peermusic III, Ltd.
International Copyright Secured   All Rights Reserved

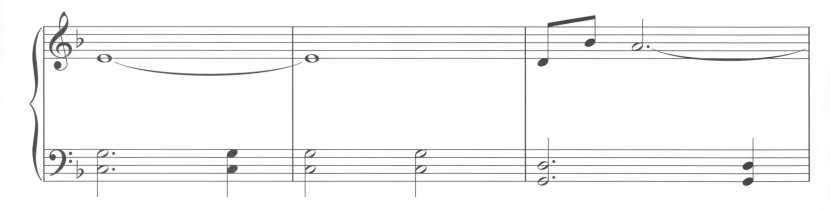

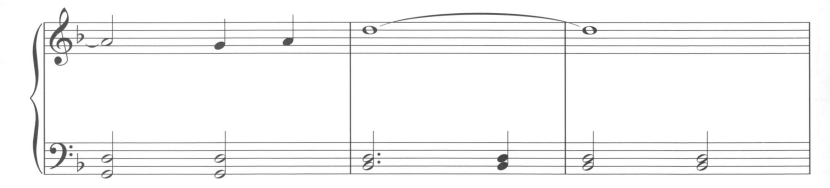

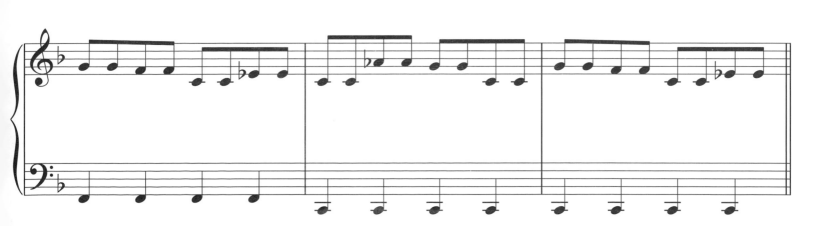

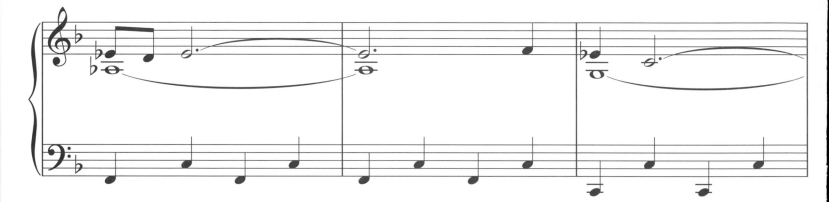

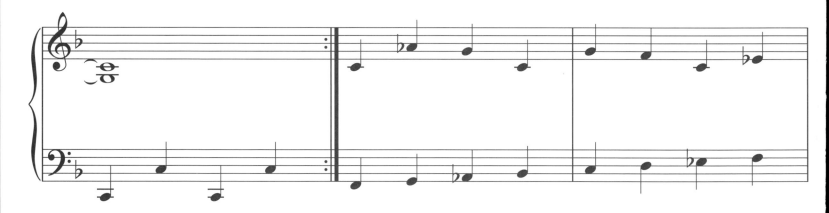

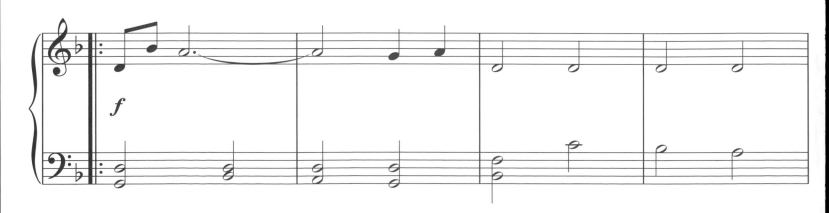

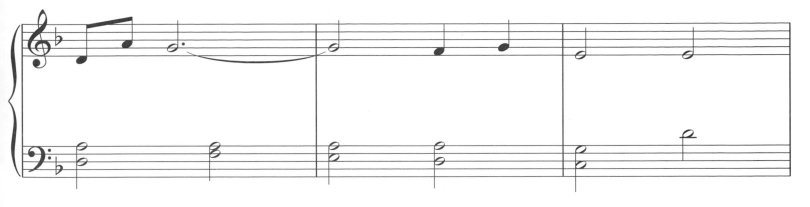

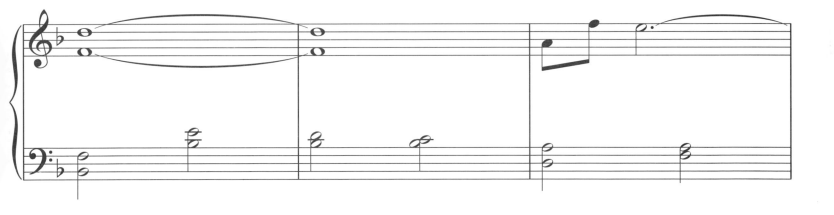

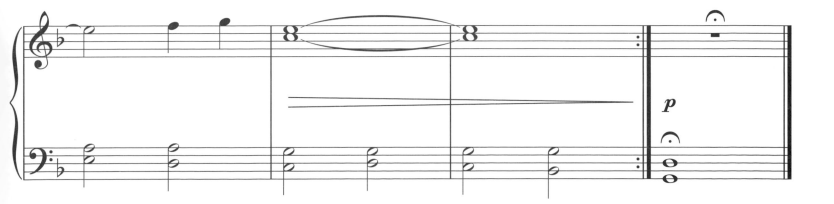

ASSASSIN'S CREED REVELATIONS

By LORNE BALFE

Slowly

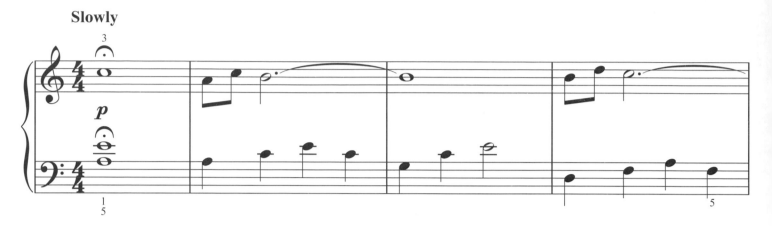

Copyright © 2011 by Ubisoft Editions Musique Inc.
All Rights in the United States Administered by Peermusic III, Ltd.
International Copyright Secured   All Rights Reserved

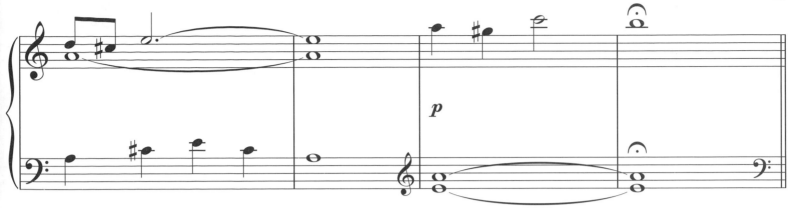

Faster

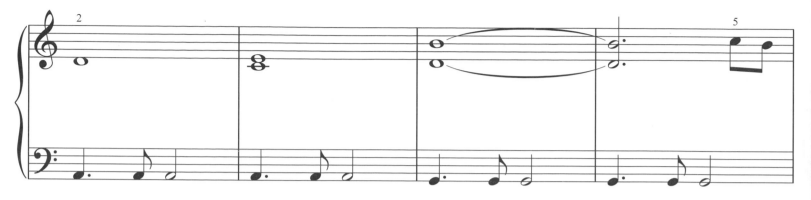

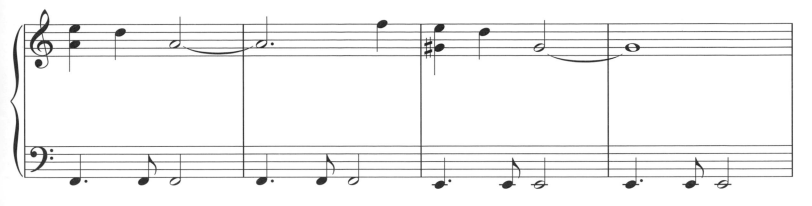

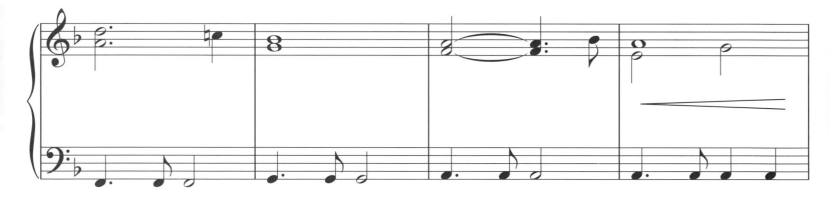

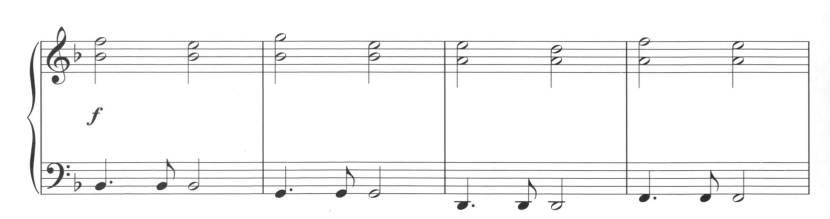

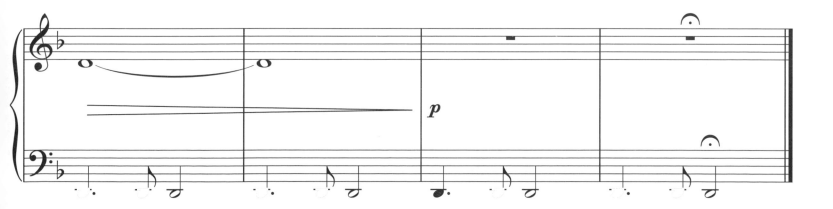

BABA YETU
from the Video Game CIVILIZATION IV

Words and Music by
CHRISTOPHER TIN

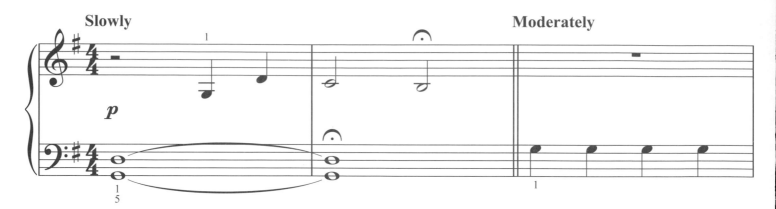

Copyright © 2005 2K Games Songs LLC
All Rights Administered by Bike Music c/o Concord Music Publishing
All Rights Reserved   Used by Permission

To Coda ⊕

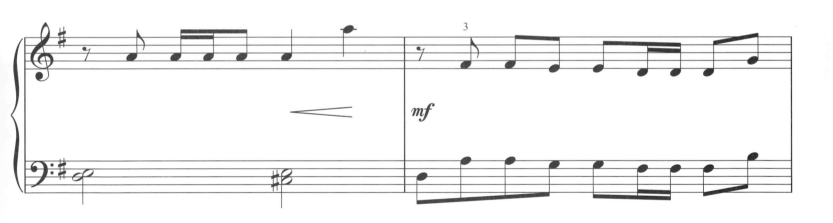

D.S. al Coda

CODA

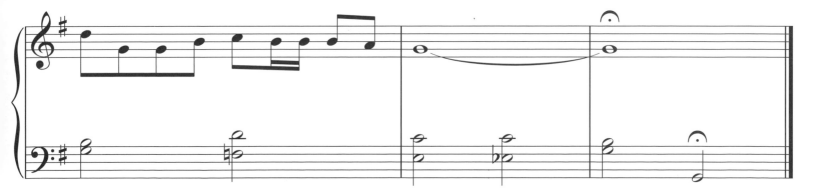

BATTLEFIELD THEME

By JOEL ERIKSSON

Fast, driving

Copyright © 2002 Electronic Arts Music, Electronic Arts Inc. and Kobalt Music Copyrights SARL
All Rights Administered Worldwide by Kobalt Songs Music Publishing
All Rights Reserved   Used by Permission

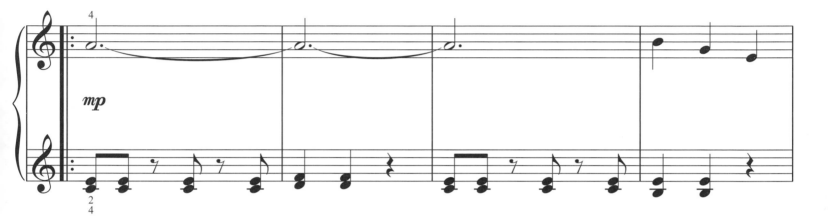

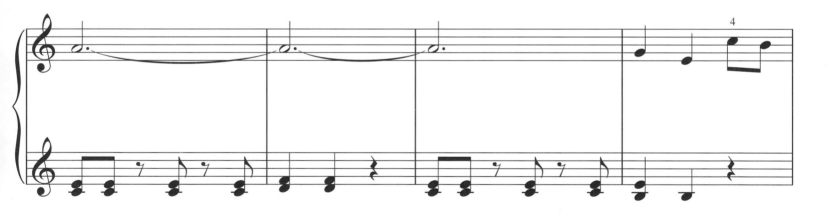

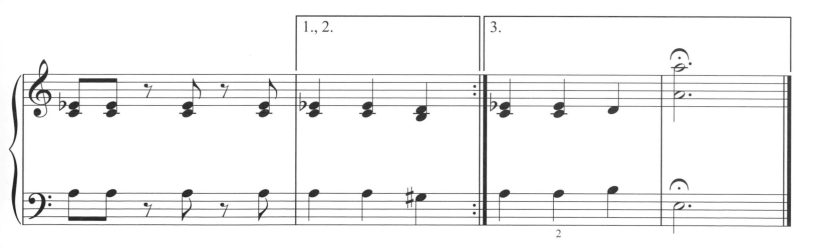

BOUNTY HUNTER
from ADVENT RISING

By TOMMY TALLARICO

Slowly

Twice as fast

Copyright © 2007 Tallarico Music Publishing
All Rights Reserved   Used by Permission

BRATJA
(Brothers)
from FULL METAL ALCHEMIST

Words and Music by MICHIRU OSHIMA,
SEIJI MIZUSHIMA and TATIANA NAUMOVA

Copyright © 2004 MYRICA MUSIC, INC.
All Rights in the U.S. and Canada Administered by UNIVERSAL - SONGS OF POLYGRAM INTERNATIONAL, INC.
All Rights Reserved   Used by Permission

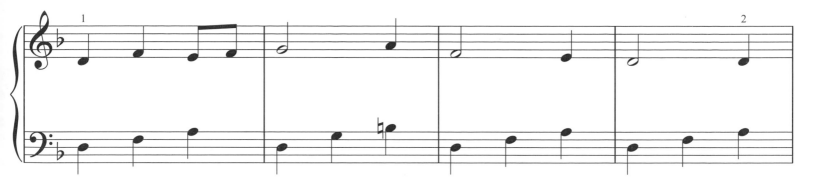

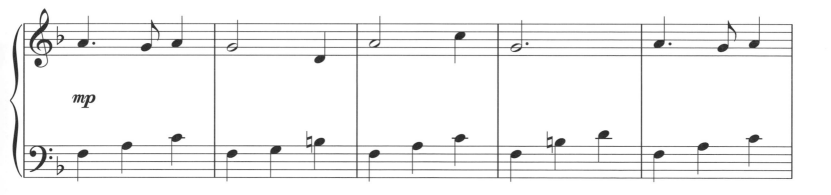

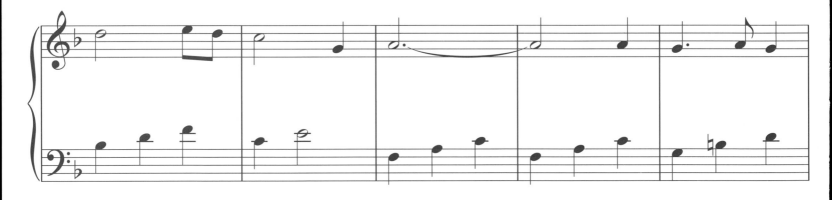

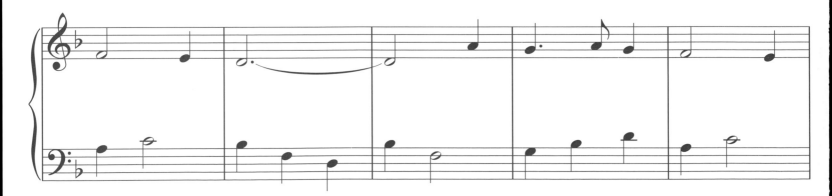

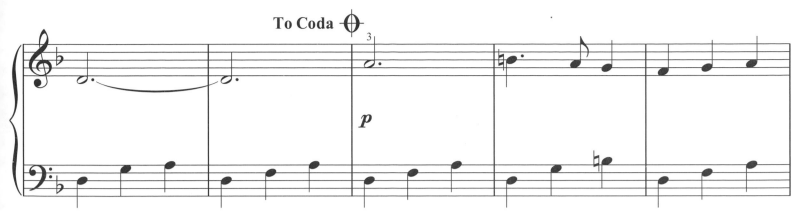

To Coda

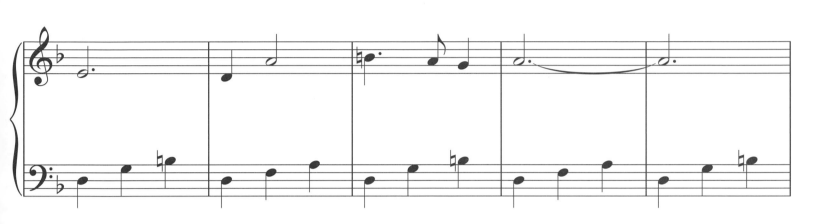

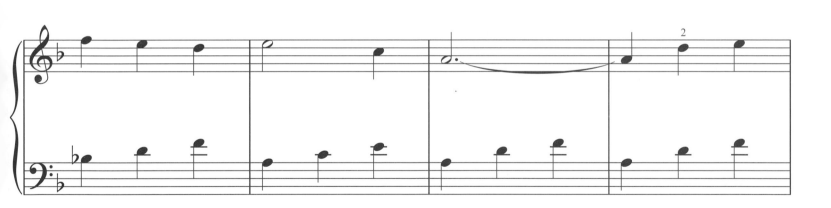

D.S. al Coda

CODA

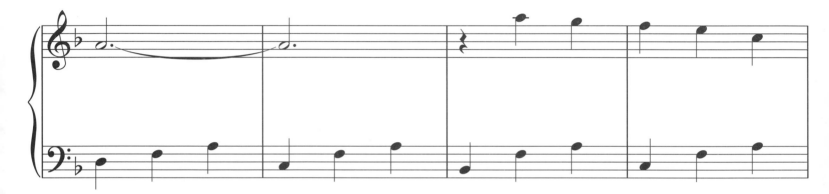

DEARLY BELOVED
from KINGDOM HEARTS

Music by
YOKO SHIMOMURA

Slowly

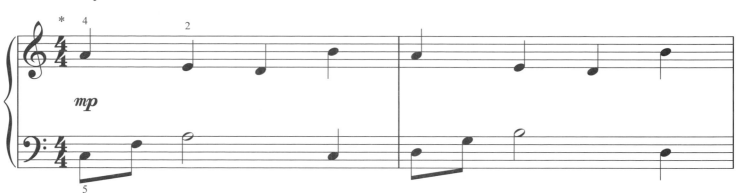

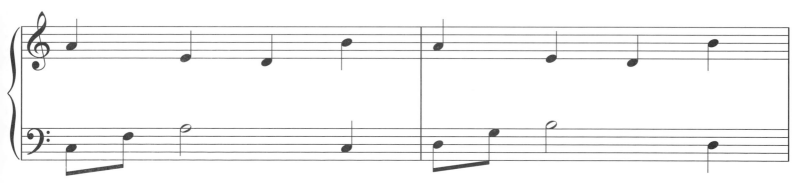

Optional: play with both hands 8va

© 2003 Walt Disney Music Company
All Rights Reserved. Used by Permission.

DON'T FORGET

from DELTARUNE™

Words and Music by
TOBY FOX

Moderately slow

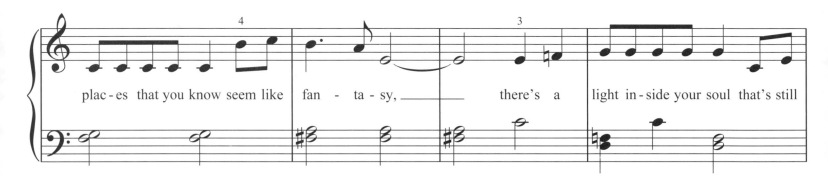

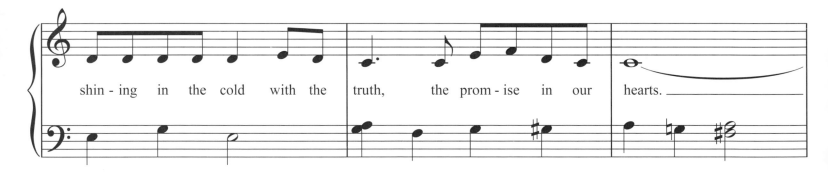

Copyright © 2018 Royal Sciences LLC (administered by MATERIA COLLECTIVE LLC)
All Rights Reserved   Used by Permission

DRAGONBORN
(Skyrim Theme)

By JEREMY SOULE

Slow and Steady

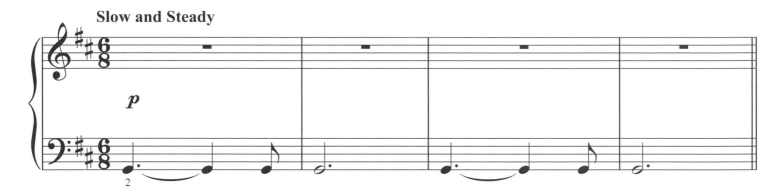

© 2011 Zenimax Music Publishing
All Rights Administered by PEN Music Group, Inc.
All Rights Reserved   Used by Permission

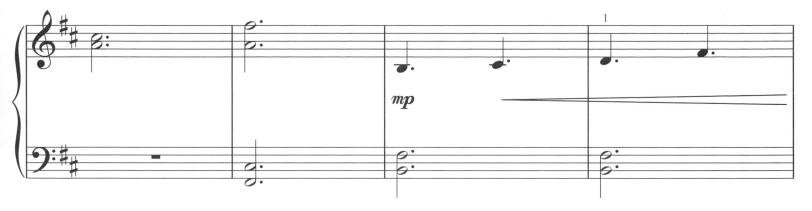

ELDER SCROLLS: OBLIVION

By JEREMY SOULE

Moderately

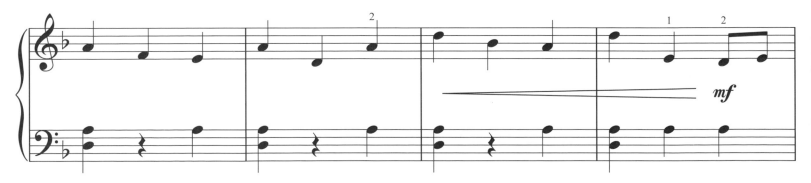

Copyright © 1994 Electronic Arts Music, Electronic Arts Inc. and Kobalt Music Copyrights SARL
All Rights Administered Worldwide by Kobalt Songs Music Publishing
All Rights Reserved   Used by Permission

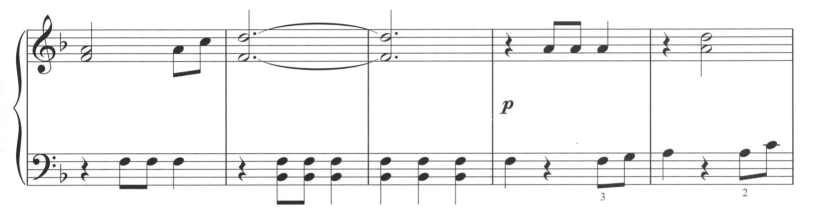

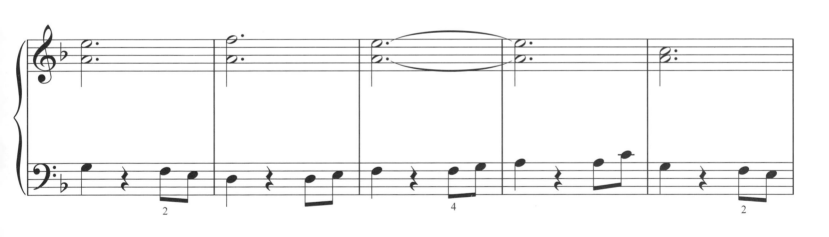

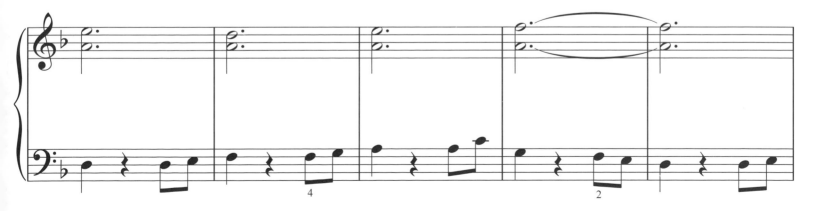

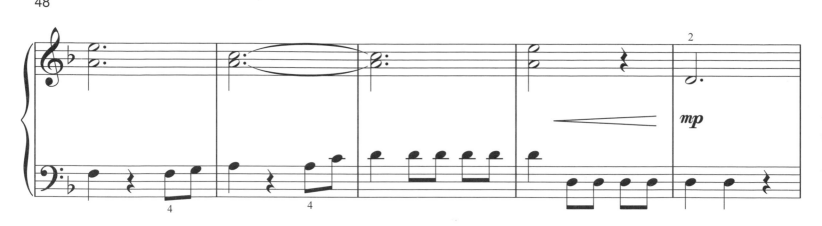

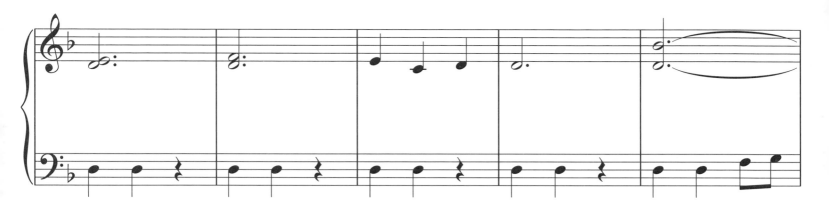

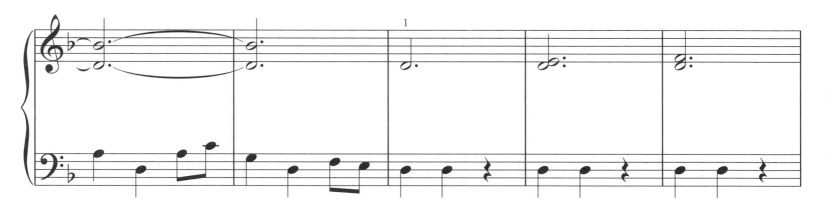

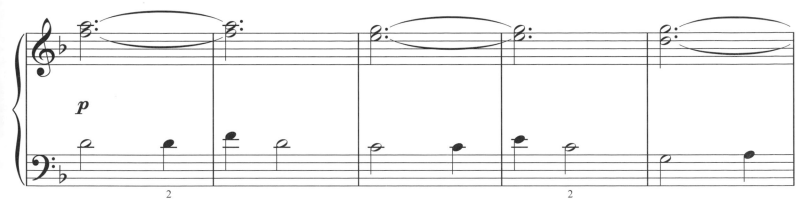

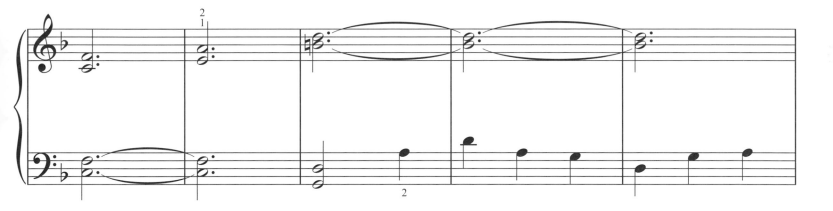

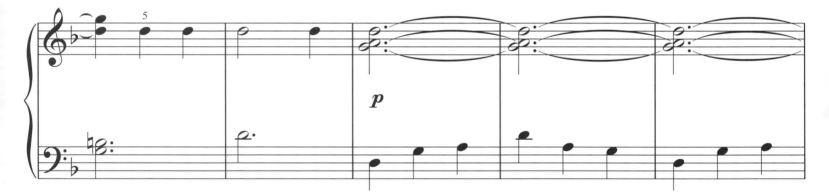

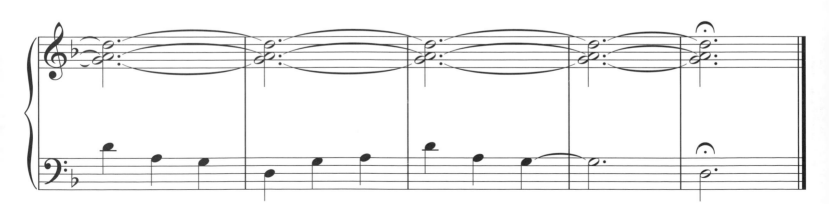

THEME FROM FALLOUT®4

Composed by INON ZUR

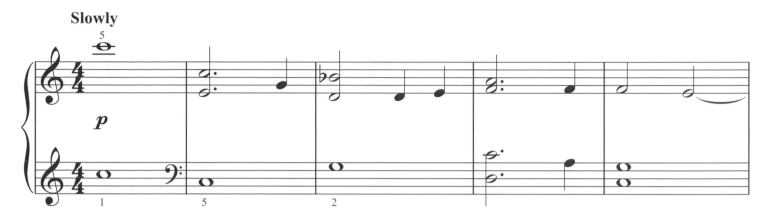

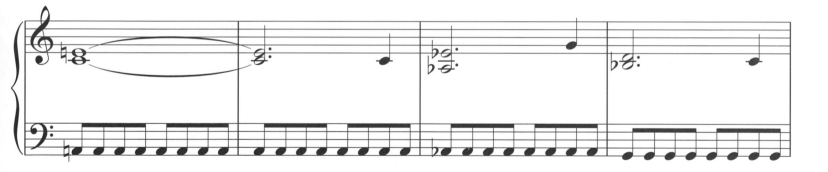

Copyright © 2015 Bethesda Softworks LLC, a Zenimax Media company
All Rights Reserved
No portion of this sheet music may be reproduced or transmitted in any form or by any means without written permission from Bethesda Softworks LLC.

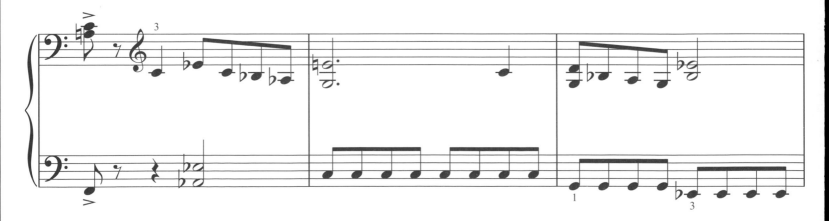

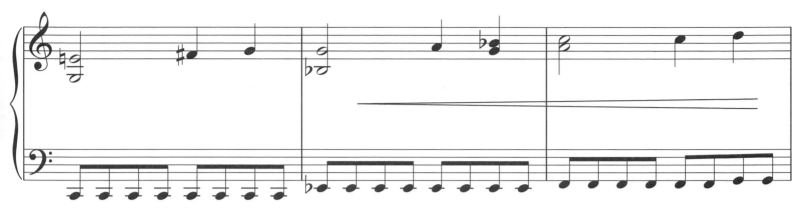

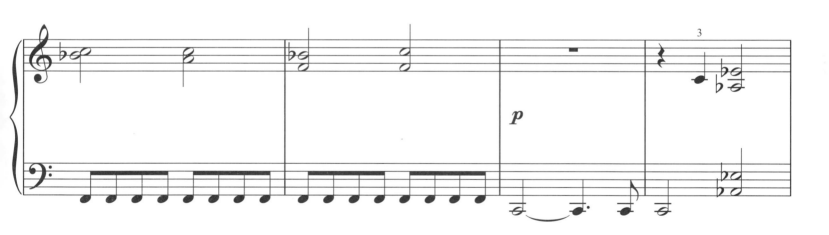

EYES ON ME
from FINAL FANTASY VIII

Music by NOBUO UEMATSU
Lyrics by KAKO SOMEYA

Moderately slow

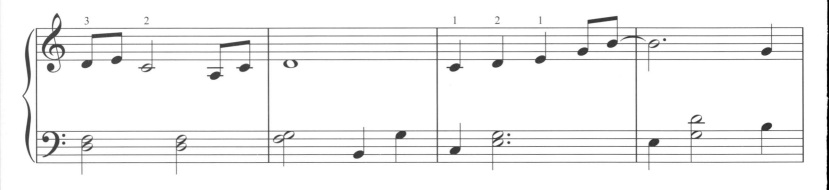

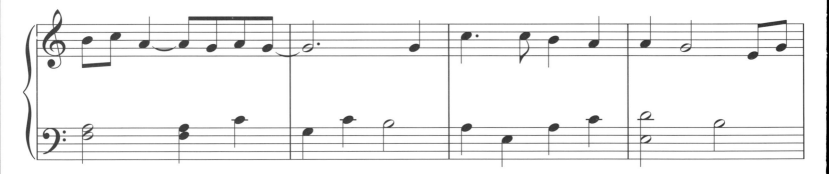

© 1999 SQUARE ENIX CO. LTD.
All Rights in the U.S. and Canada Administered by WB MUSIC CORP.
All Rights Reserved   Used by Permission

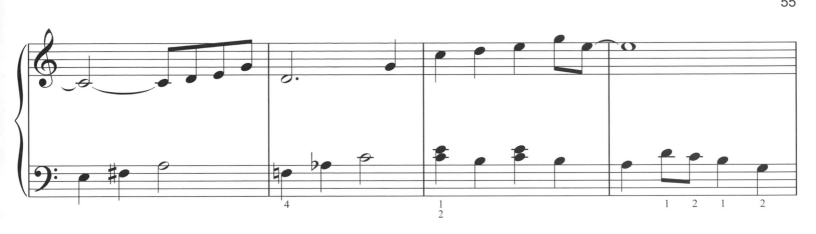

MAIN THEME
from FINAL FANTASY I

By NOBUO UEMATSU

Moderately

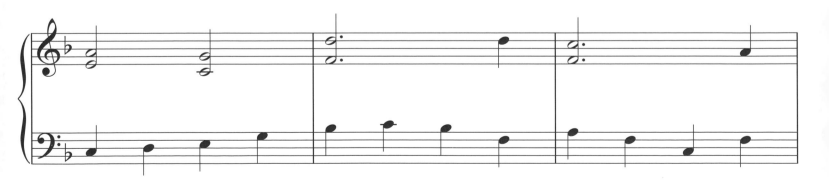

© 1987 SQUARE ENIX CO. LTD.
All Rights in the U.S. and Canada Administered by WB MUSIC CORP.
All Rights Reserved   Used by Permission

MAIN THEME
from FINAL FANTASY VII

By NOBOU UEMATSU

© 1997 SQUARE ENIX CO. LTD.
All Rights in the U.S. and Canada Administered by WB MUSIC CORP.
All Rights Reserved   Used by Permission

To Coda ⊕

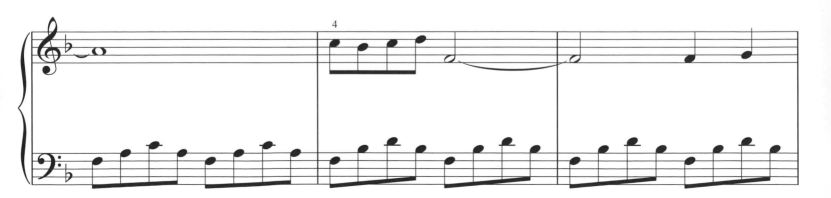

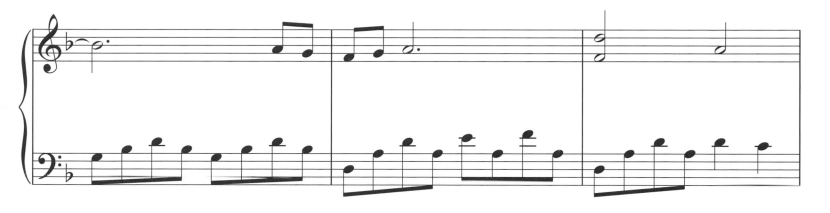

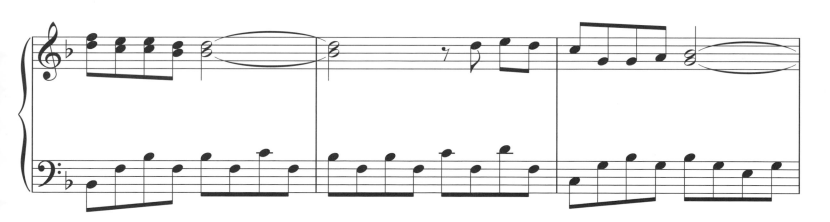

D.S. al Coda

CODA

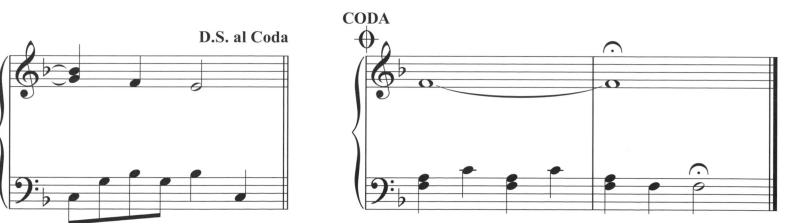

OVERTURE
from GOD OF WAR III

By GERARD MARINO

Moderately fast

Copyright © 2010 Sony Interactive Entertainment LLC
All Rights Reserved   Used by Permission

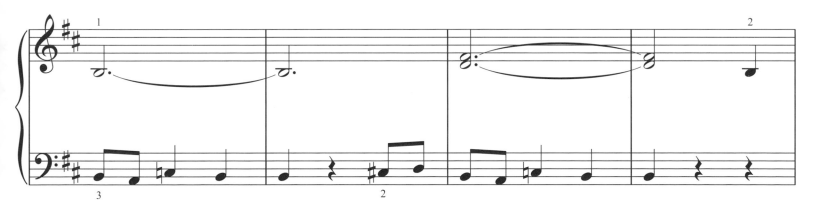

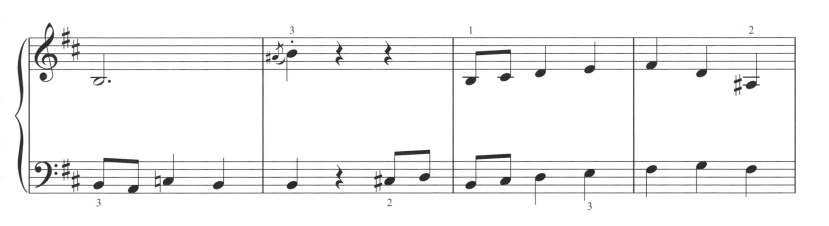

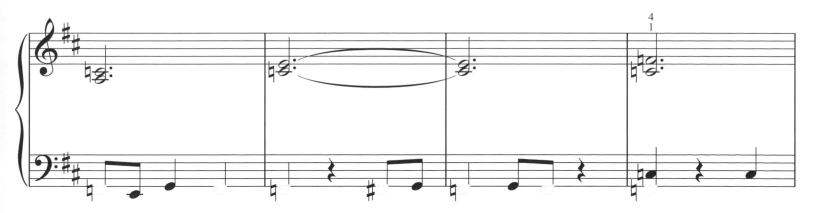

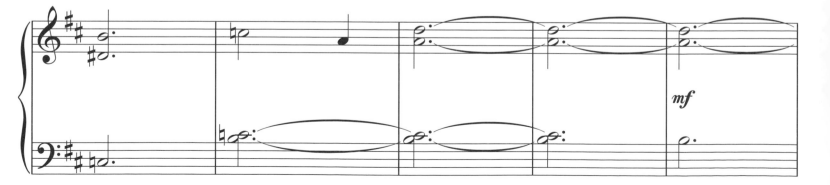

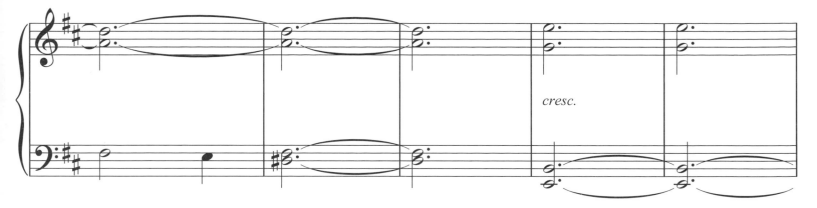

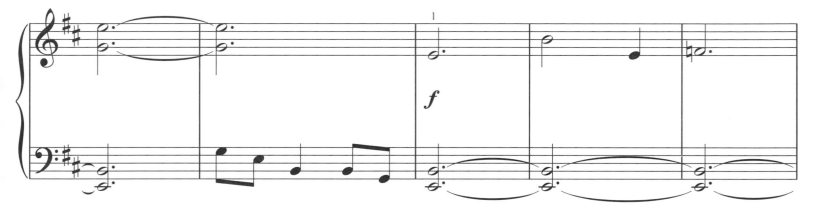

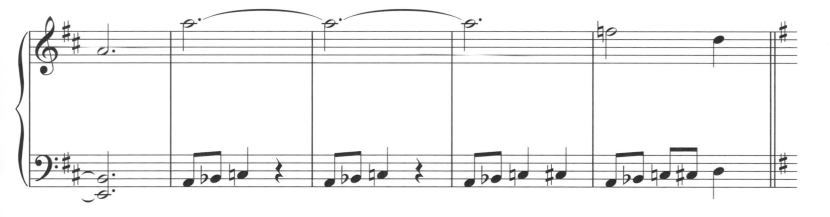

Slow and heavy

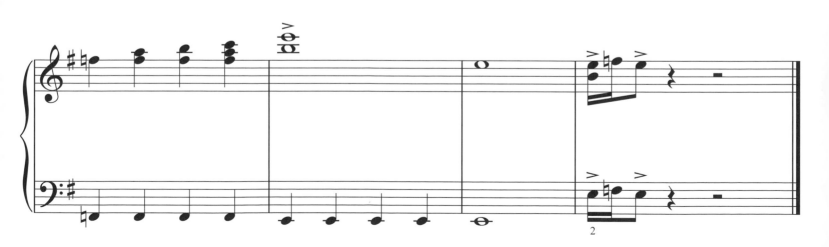

THE LAST OF US

By GUSTAVO SANTAOLALLA

Copyright © 2013 Sony Interactive Entertainment LLC
All Rights Reserved   Used by Permission

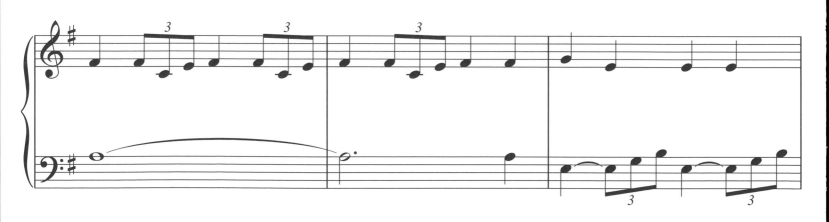

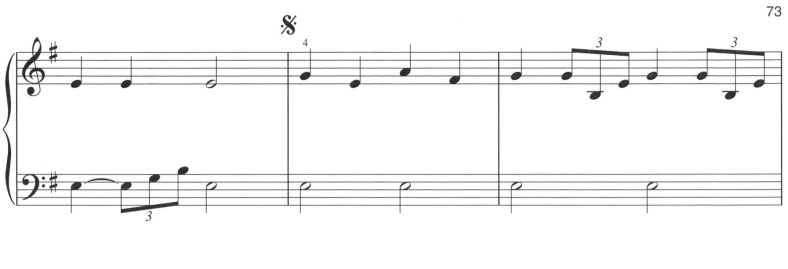

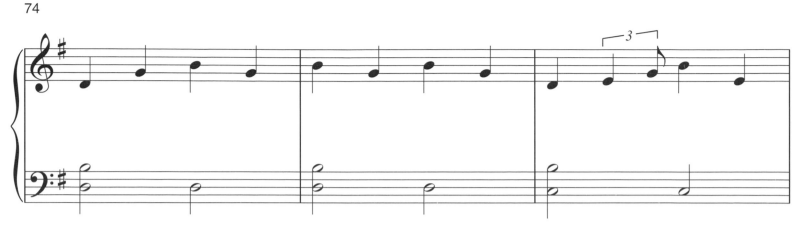

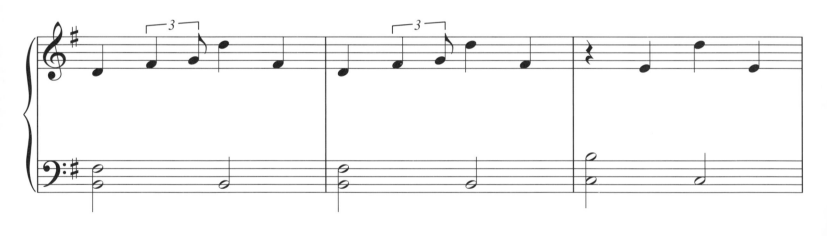

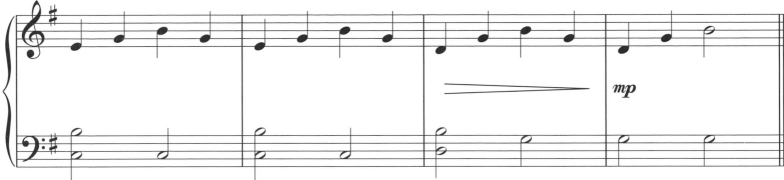

CODA

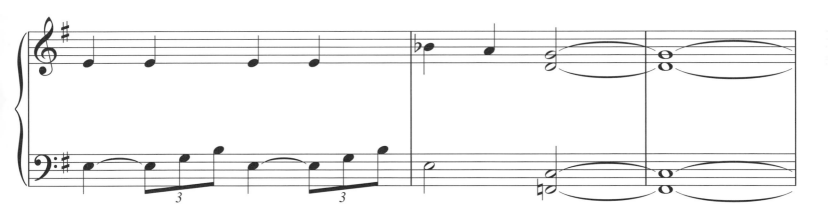

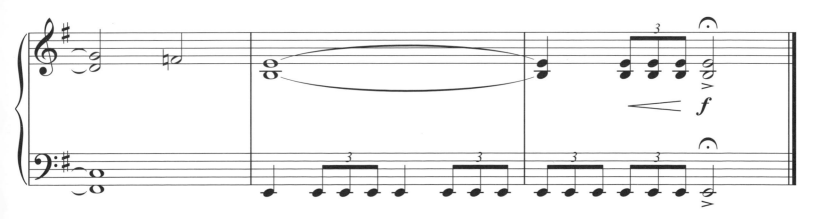

MAIN THEME
from THE LONG DARK: WINTERMUTE

By CRIS VELASCO

Slowly

Copyright © 2017 Hinterland Studio Inc.
All Rights Reserved   Used by Permission

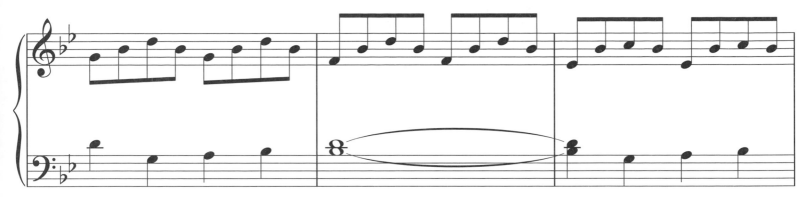

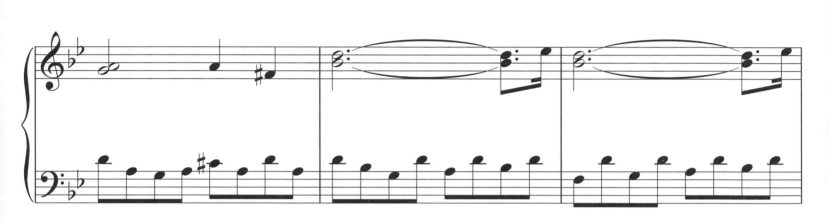

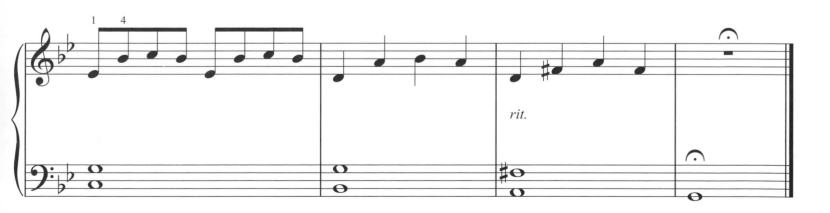

MASS EFFECT: SUICIDE MISSION

By SAM HULICK
and JACK WALL

Moderately fast

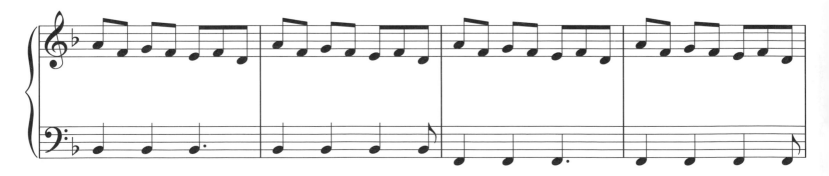

Copyright © 2010 Electronic Arts Music, Electronic Arts Inc. and Kobalt Music Copyrights SARL
All Rights Administered Worldwide by Kobalt Songs Music Publishing
All Rights Reserved   Used by Permission

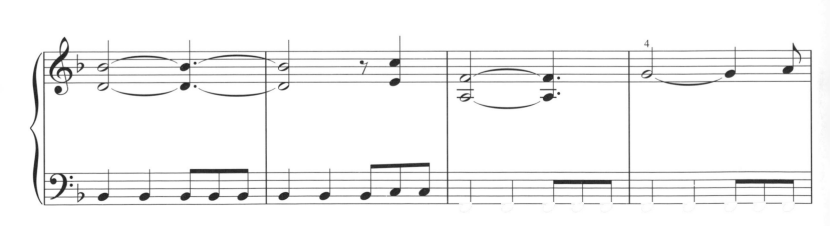

MEGALOVANIA
from UNDERTALE®

Music by
TOBY FOX

Moderately

Copyright © 2015 Royal Sciences LLC (administered by Materia Collective LLC)
All Rights Reserved   Used by Permission

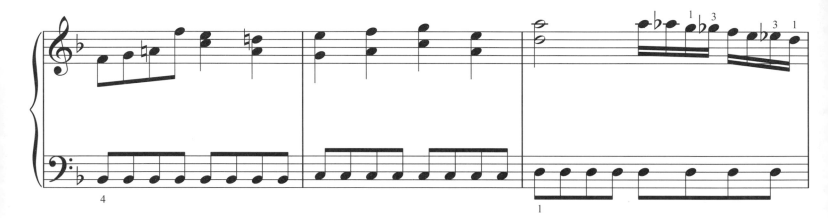

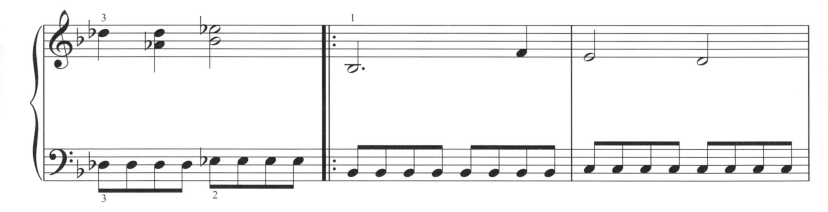

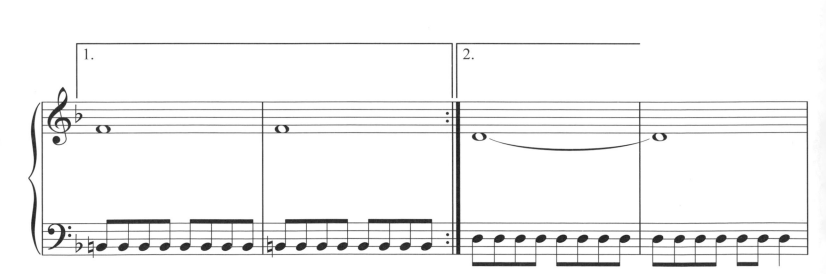

METAL GEAR SOLID-SONS OF LIBERTY

By HARRY GREGSON-WILLIAMS

Moderately fast

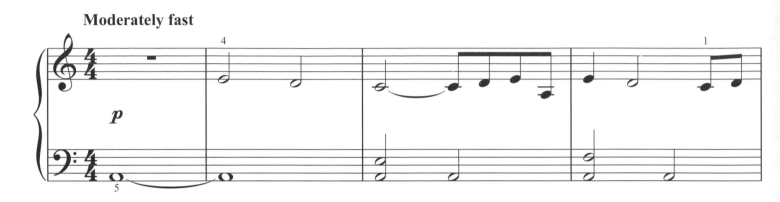

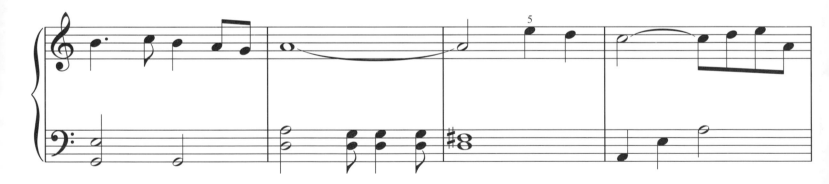

Copyright © 2001 Un Jazz Music
All Rights Reserved   Used by Permission

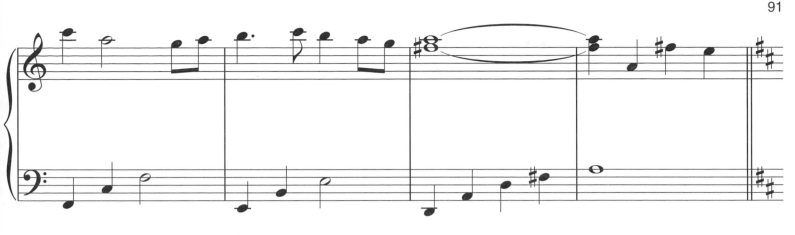

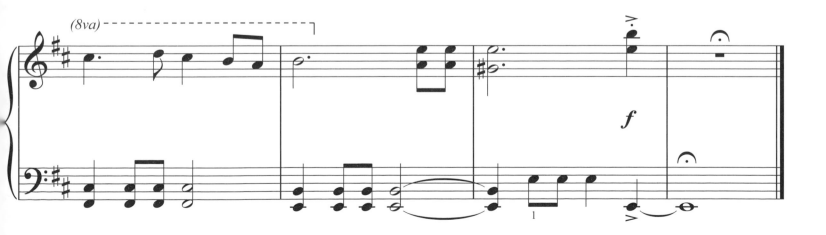

MINECRAFT: SWEDEN

By DANIEL ROSENFELD

Very slowly

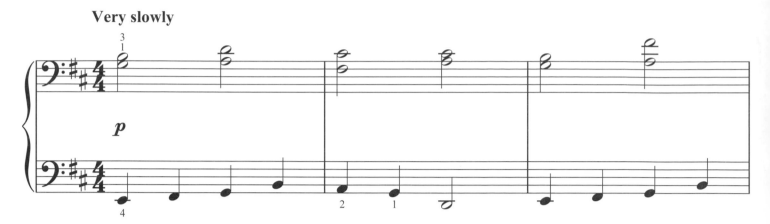

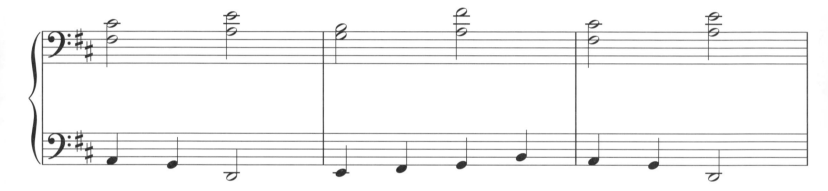

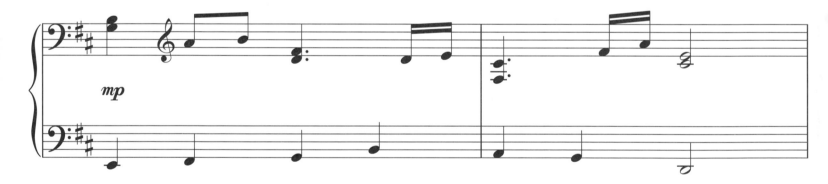

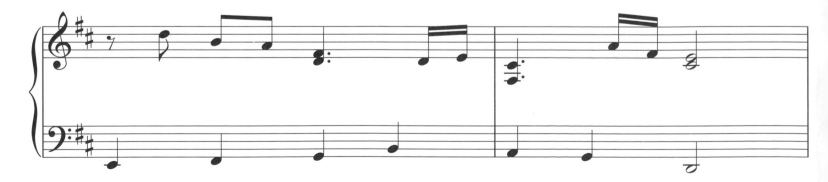

Copyright © 2011 Tunecore Digital Music
All Rights Reserved   Used by Permission

MUSE
from ADVENT RISING

By TOMMY TALLARICO

Slowly

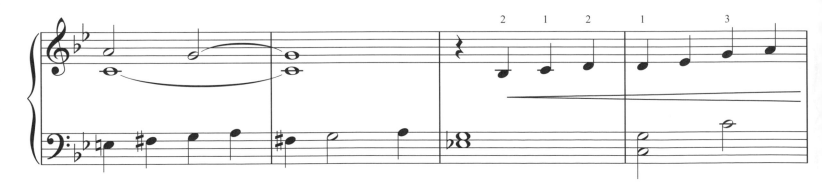

Copyright © 2007 Tallarico Music Publishing
All Rights Reserved   Used by Permission

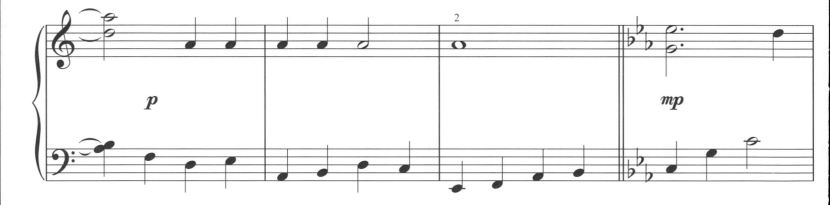

RAGE OF SPARTA
from GOD OF WAR III

By GERARD MARINO

Moderately

Copyright © 2010 Sony Interactive Entertainment LLC
All Rights Reserved   Used by Permission

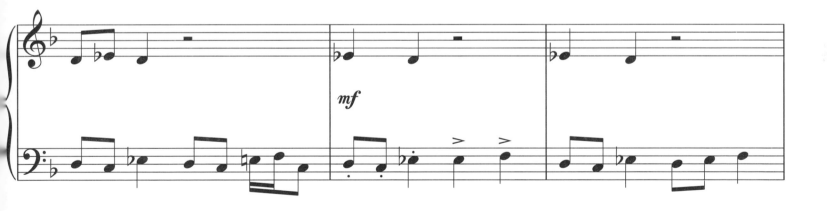

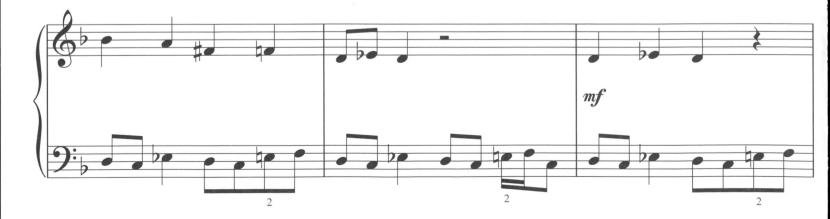

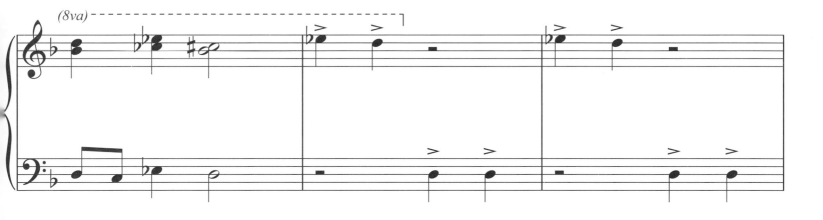

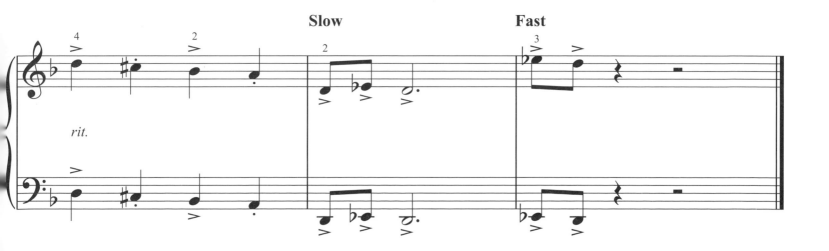

SADNESS AND SORROW
from the television series NARUTO

By PUROJEKUTO MUSASHI

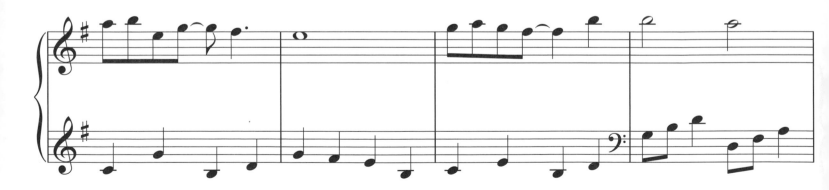

Copyright © 2002 TV Tokyo Music, Inc.
All Rights Administered by Sony/ATV Music Publishing LLC, 424 Church Street, Suite 1200, Nashville, TN 37219
International Copyright Secured   All Rights Reserved

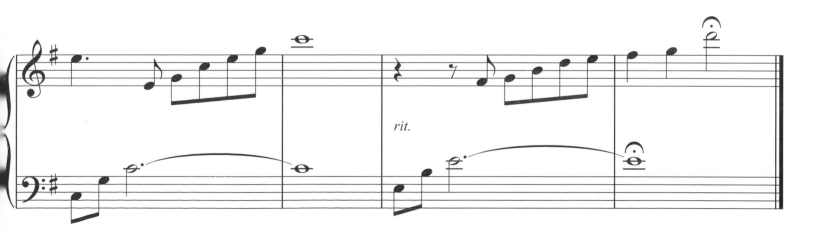

SPLINTER CELL: CONVICTION

Words and Music by KAVEH COHEN
and MICHAEL NIELSEN

Moderately slow

© 2010 PYRO PROMO MUSIC
All Rights Administered by GROOVE ADDICTS OUTRAGEOUS MUSIC
All Rights Reserved   Used by Permission

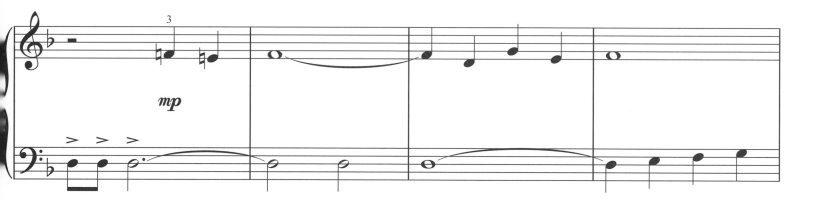

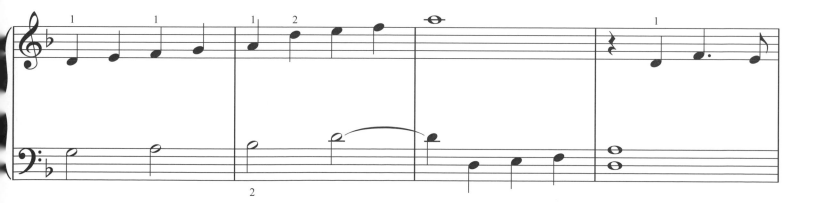

UNCHARTED: NATE'S THEME
from UNCHARTED: DRAKE'S FORTUNE

By GREG EDMONDSON

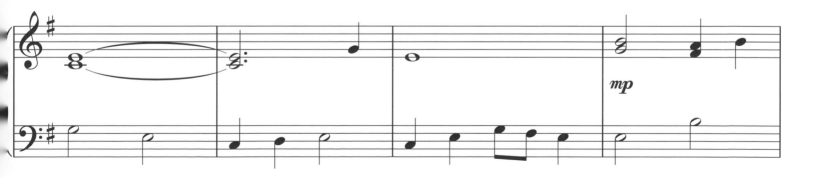

Copyright © 2007 Sony Interactive Entertainment LLC
All Rights Reserved   Used by Permission

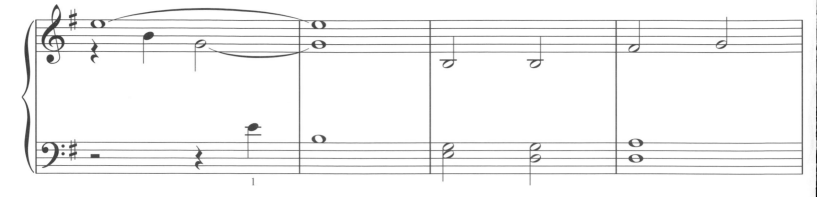

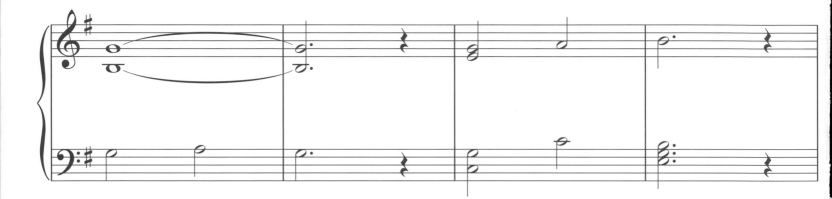

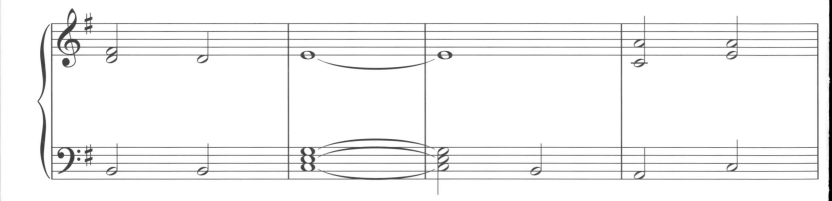

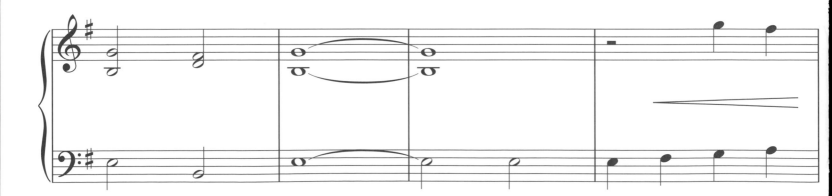

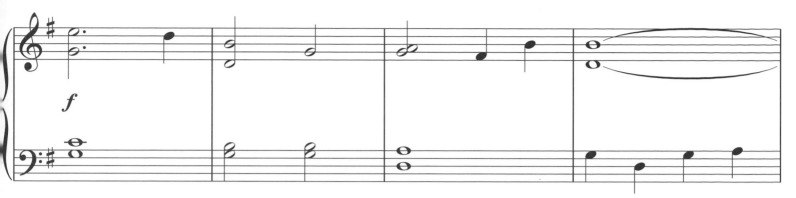

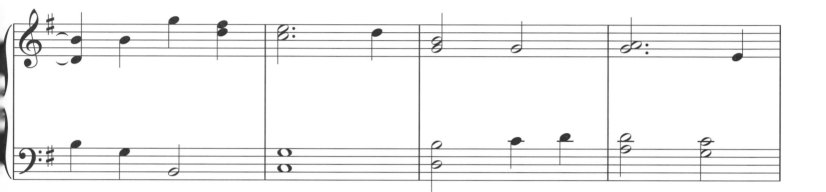

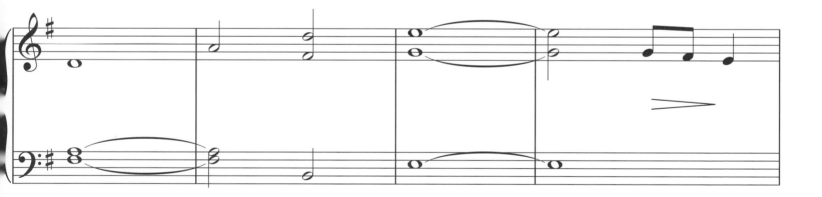

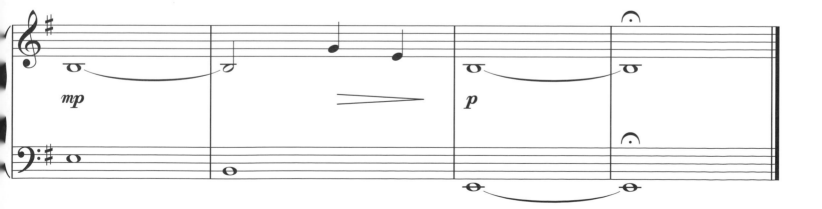

UNCHARTED THEME
from UNCHARTED: DRAKE'S FORTUNE

By GREG EDMONSON

Moderately

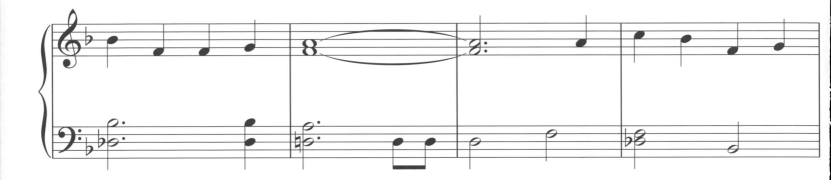

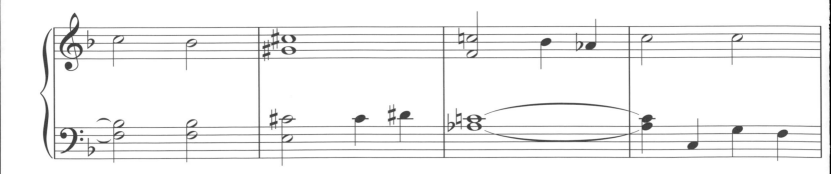

Copyright © 2007 Sony Interactive Entertainment LLC
All Rights Reserved   Used by Permission

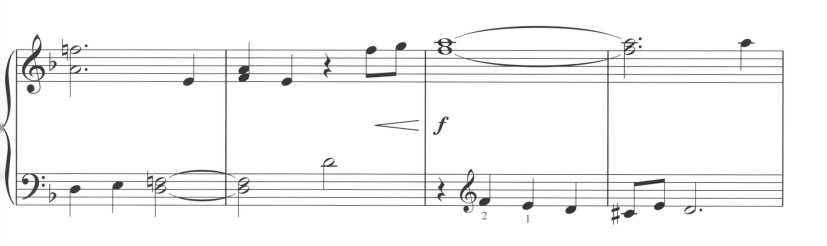

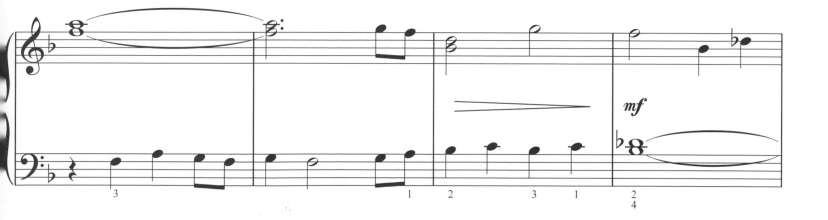

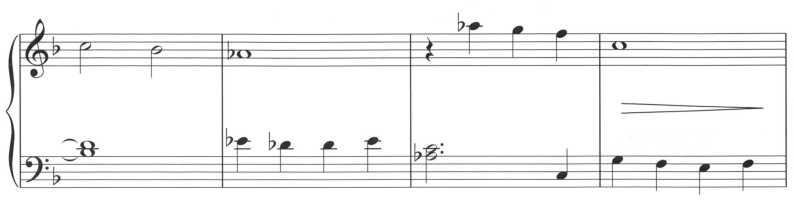

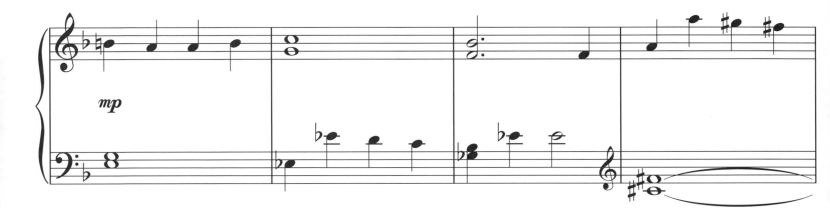

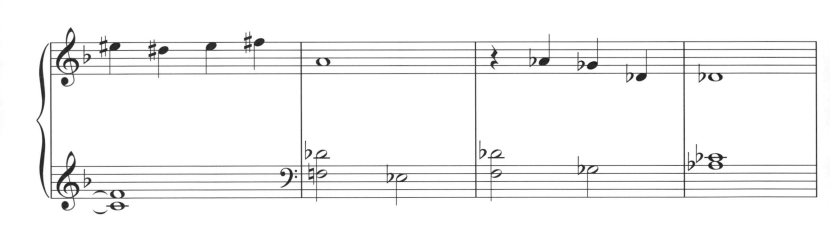

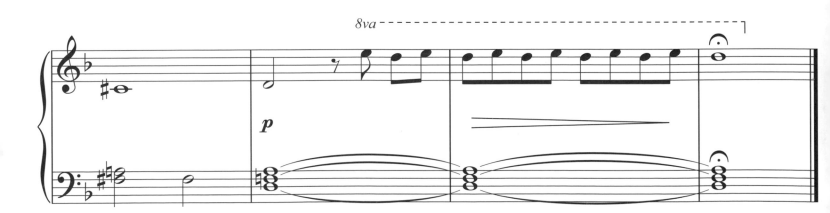